CONTENTS

Introduction

I have found, throughout my creative endeavours in writing and styling, that the overlooked and the un-fashionable often illuminate and inform the way. The temptation is always to look in front of us or towards what everyone else is staring at. But setting our gaze to the middle distance offers a rich stylistic trove. There is glamour and grace everywhere - it is just that our eyes, en masse, are not generally looking in that direction.

Flowers have been studied for centuries - academically and in close admiration. In turn, the shamelessly wonderful talent of botanical illustration, popularized by the Victorians, still resonates today with both botanists and general observers. Those images have become etched on our cultural consciousness, from tissued sheets in valuable museum tomes, to reproduction prints on our mothers' and grandmothers' bedroom walls.

Our aim in this anthology is to present images that are intricate and imbued with detailed realism. Set against the bedrock of cultural and historical reference, these interpretations open the way to truly see and feel enriched by the splendour that is around us in the world - in our gardens, window boxes, flower shops, parks and collections.

Anthology of
FLOWERS

Anthology of
FLOWERS

Words by Jane Field-Lewis
Photography by Richard Maxted

quadrille

"There are always flowers for those who want to see them."

Henri Matisse

These are not phone snaps, well filtered, but the opposite end of the digital photography spectrum. Looking at the larger format, hauntingly beautiful images emerge, the process slow, considered, focused – the result of the interplay of human and technical skills. Open this book at any page, and you may think you are admiring a painting, but this is the truest reproduction of a flower.

We have cast a very modern light upon these delicate creatures. By illuminating their intense beauty, and observing minutely their form, texture, colour and sense, we've attempted to reveal their very being through photography and words.

Look closely, and enjoy really seeing.

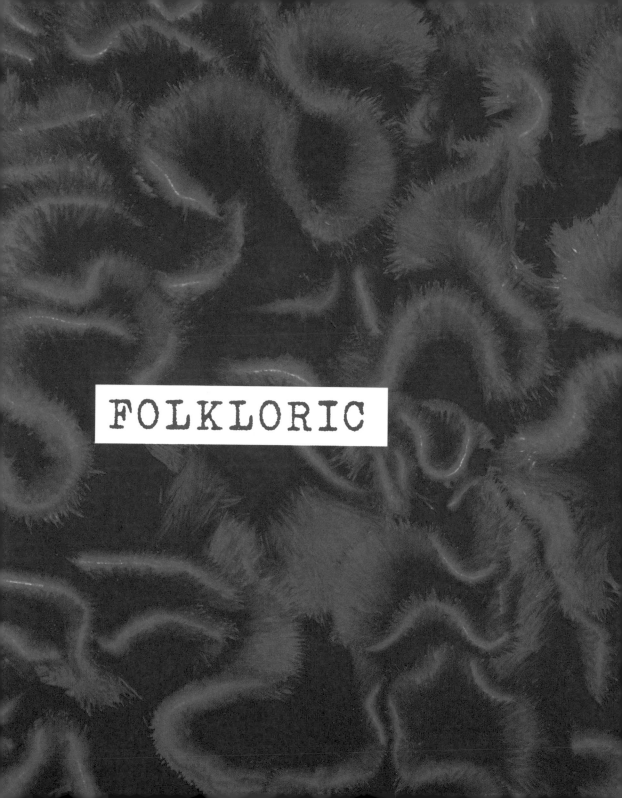

FOLKLORIC

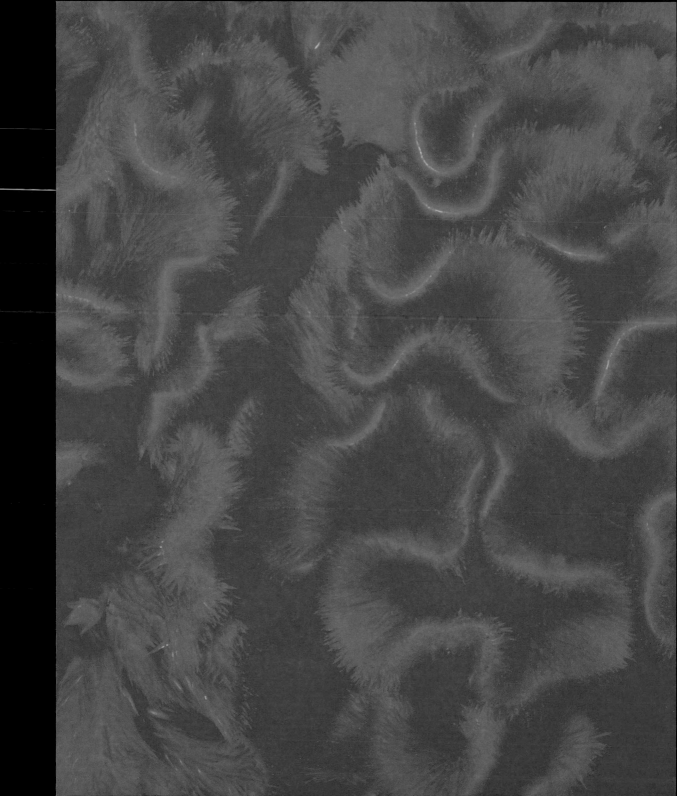

Stargazer lily

It's been dubbed a floral celebrity for its striking good looks and, in plant terms, its relative youth, having only been introduced in the 1970s. The stargazer is a hybrid lily of the Oriental group, specially adapted so its blooms face skywards but still retaining the perfume of its cousins.

Part of its popularity with the flower-buying public is the stargazer's ability to rise to almost any occasion. Need to say sorry? The stargazer can. Congratulations? Its associations with aspiration, wealth and prosperity should do the trick nicely.

It can also call on the lily family's wealth of cultural and religious symbolism over the centuries, from ancient Greece, where it was linked to sexuality, to early Christian paintings, where it represented chastity and purity. It crops up in folklore, too, especially in determining the sex of an unborn child.

Nowadays the flower has made common parlance. We talk about "gilding the lily" to refer to unnecessary ornamentation or over-embellishment because it is viewed as a benchmark for idealism and flawlessness. Nothing, William Blake once wrote, can "stain her beauty bright".

Cockscomb

It is a shame that a flower that looks like the human brain should suffer the indignity of a long association with silliness and the absurd. That is the fate of the vividly coloured, curiously contorted cockscomb bloom, whose name suggests how it acquired the ridiculous connotations of the rooster's crown, an infinitely less than cerebral mass.

In Asian cultures it carries more weighty and propitious undertones. Shen Zhou, a Ming dynasty painter, depicted the flower in ink on paper – alongside a cockerel – to hint at imminent promotion. The flower-and-fowl combination suggests high positions and handsome salaries.

Neighbouring Japan has also taken the cockscomb to its heart: the online collection of the Metropolitan Museum of Art features a stunning kimono from the Taisho period decorated with burnt-orange cockscomb flowers. Their vibrancy on the kimono tempts one to reach out and touch their uniquely velvety flowerheads. No surprise, then, that in Mexico the cockscomb is affectionately known as the "velvet flower".

Lady's mantle

The Cinderella of flowers, lady's mantle (*alchemilla*) spends most of its time in service. Gardeners find it useful en masse for groundcover or edging paths. Nothing glamorous then, but it seems to cheerfully accept its lot, putting up with some pretty horrible conditions in the process, including heavy clay and, once established, drought, too.

Healers have also put it to work – to treat a variety of conditions, both internal and external, painful and mild. Gargled, it is even said to soothe a sore throat or mouth.

It's not all drudgery and beneficence for the *alchemilla*, however. After heavy rain it becomes almost unrecognizable thanks to a clever ability to catch and hold water droplets. Thus bejewelled – like a lady's mantle – the effect is mesmerizing. Think of Rihanna's infamous Adam Selman gown at the CFDA fashion awards made of 230,000 Swarovski crystals, and you have some idea how breathtaking its scalloped green leaves look against a cloud of tiny chartreuse flowers. Alchemists considered these beads to be the purest form of water and harvested it in their attempt to turn base metal into gold, giving the plant its magical name.

Cyclamen

It is said that the cyclamen can raise self-esteem and confidence. Come winter, its flame-like upswept petals – like so many candles on a birthday cake – are certainly cheering, providing a welcome splash of colour when little else is flowering.

Poets D.H. Lawrence and William Carlos Williams were fascinated by these diminutive plants, both men imbuing them with drama and something distinctly primal. Williams described "an ecstasy" of unfurling petals held aloft, while Lawrence saw something more sinister in the "muzzles together, ears a-prick, whispering witchcraft".

He wasn't the only one to be unsettled by these blooms. Folklore warns women in the early stages of pregnancy to give them a wide berth lest walking past or over them cause miscarriage. Worn in labour, however, the flowers could purportedly come in handy by speeding the delivery.

Folklore and remedy being inextricably linked, the cyclamen was believed to provide purgative relief of various kinds – another boon from this cheering flower.

Dandelion

It's the shape-shifter of the flower world: one moment a bright sun of yellow petals, another a ghostly full moon of silver-haired seed heads that hitchhike huge distances on the back of a breeze. As children, we hold the flowers as divining rods under our chins to check for a golden glow of future riches. The seed heads are equally entrancing. We blow them to tell the time, or if we're loved by a partner, or to determine how many children we'll have. Sometimes we wish on them.

The name comes from the French *dent-de-lion*, meaning "lion's tooth", an allusion to the incisor-like serrations of the plant's leaves. In fact, unsettling connotations like this are few and far between. In a wedding bouquet, for example, a dandelion brings good luck, while buried in the northwest corner of a house it will summon favourable winds.

At the seed-head stage, dandelions make fine meteorologists. Extended to the full? You can count on a fine day. If the pappus hairs close in on themselves it'd be wise to have an umbrella to hand. Or, take a sip of dandelion tea – it's supposed to boost psychic abilities and could help you spot next week's low pressure system in advance of the weatherman.

Snapdragon

This most multi-sensory of plants got its name from the peculiar way the flowers, when pressed, open and close like a mouth. While the English see in them a dragon's jaws, other cultures have drawn similarities with different creatures. In Holland they are known as "lion's lips", while in Asia they bear the rather less fearsome nickname of "rabbit's lips".

Curiously, the snapdragon's botanical name, *antirrhinum*, refers to another facial feature entirely – the nose – presumably for the snout-like look of the flowers. Snapdragons, which come in an array of cheerful colours, start blooming at the bottom of the stalk and work their way up to produce clusters of as many as 15 blooms.

A relation of the foxglove, snapdragons symbolize both graciousness and deception, and were once believed to offer protection from witchcraft. In the dramatic poem that bears their name, meanwhile, D.H. Lawrence uses the flowers to show how closely love and cruelty are entwined. The narrator is asked to throttle a bloom for his sweetheart's entertainment, "and the flower gaped wide with woe". It's a captivating poem that will prompt the reader to view these "dragon's jaws" in a new light.

MEDICINAL

Clematis

"In a month there will be purple stars on the clematis, and year after year the green night of its leaves will hold its purple stars. But we never get back our youth."

In *The Picture of Dorian Gray*, Oscar Wilde uses this flower, among others, to distinguish between the short-lived beauty of man and nature's ability to regenerate. He chose his analogy well, because there are few plants to match a clematis's wealth of colour, floral exhibitionism and downright gorgeousness.

A climbing plant, the clematis has its origins in the Far East, but it was the American Old West that cultivated it for more than its exotic good looks. There, the plant was admired for its medicinal qualities, including relief of headaches, skin infections and nervous disorders. The seeds and leaves were selected as a substitute for pepper – but with caution, because large amounts were known to cause internal bleeding.

Few people take this risk nowadays, and the clematis is instead called upon to spice up fabric, wallpaper and crockery designs, where its large, simplistic shape lends itself well to pattern work.

Matriciana chamomilla

Chamomile is the chameleon of the herbal medicine cupboard. It has been touted as a cure for everything from coughs and skin inflammation to liver and gallbladder complaints, taking in hay fever and muscle spasms along the way. Your grandmother may even tell you a cup of chamomile tea before sleep will stop you from having nightmares. Beatrix Potter certainly thought a lot of it, ensuring her best-loved children's character, Peter Rabbit, was given "a dose of it" and sent to bed when he was feeling unwell.

The daisy-like flower can be found across Europe and temperate Asia, and it isn't picky about choosing a home – roadsides and landfill sites are often chamomile hotbeds. This is good news for things already growing in those areas, because it's not for nothing that chamomile is known as the "plant's physician". Grow it near a drooping or sickly plant, and its restorative powers can be quite astounding.

Physalis

The physalis – or Chinese lantern – berry and its papery cape are oft-admired but rarely eaten with the cheesecake they decorate. Diners seem suspicious of them. That's a shame, because they bring with them dietary goodness, including healthy helpings of beta-carotene, vitamins B and C and, unusually for a fruit, protein, too. It should be eaten only when ripe, as it is toxic before then.

In addition to being a nutritious snack, the physalis is reputed to have medicinal properties, although it is rarely used in modern practice. Past prescriptions have been as a diuretic, antiseptic, liver corrective and sedative. The seed has also been used to promote early labour.

The berries supersede white, five-petalled flowers that bloom in summer. However, it is the novelty "lanterns" shading the fruit in autumn that make the physalis so popular, especially because their appearance coincides with Thanksgiving and Halloween celebrations. They're a festival favourite in Japan, too, where the seeds are used as offerings as part of Bon – the Buddhist-Confucian rite honouring ancestral spirits.

Lily of the valley

Observant royalists will recognise the delicate bell-shaped flowers of lily of the valley as part of Kate Middleton's bridal bouquet in 2011. Grace Kelly also chose the sweetly scented bloom for hers. Strange then, that the flower is more traditionally associated with female sorrow. Christian stories abound of the plant springing out of soil watered by the Virgin Mary's tears on seeing her son crucified, or by Eve's sobs at having been driven from the Garden of Eden. Its common name in Bulgarian and Macedonian is the poignant "lass's tear".

The Victorians put a more positive spin on lily of the valley, seeing it as the signifier of a return to happiness. This change in fortune spread to France at the beginning of the twentieth century, where it was sold on 1 May as a symbol of spring.

No one appreciates this calming plant more, however, than patients with cardio-vascular problems. Although toxic in large doses, lily of the valley is used medicinally to help the heart beat more slowly, regularly and efficiently, while its strong diuretic properties lower blood pressure.

Snowberry

This most tactile of plants is more easily recognized by its white berries ("ghostberries", to some) in autumn than the small clusters of pink flowers it produces in summer. Tread on the berry, and it makes a satisfying crack underfoot; break it open by hand, and you'll marvel at the wintry scene inside – the fruit resembles fine snow.

Native Americans found a practical use for the snowberry, using it as a skin wash after discovering it can kill body parasites and hasten the healing of wounds. In Russia, the berries are still employed as a soothing folk-remedy hand lotion. Ingesting them is less smart – snowberries can cause mild symptoms of vomiting, dizziness, and even slight sedation in children.

Dill

A Pollyanna of a plant, dill's natural disposition seems to be both cheerful and useful. The flowers themselves, shaped like pretty parasols, are composed of a multitude of sunny yellow blossoms and are becoming firm favourites with florists as airy fillers in bouquets.

Dill is helpful in the home dispensary, too. Traditionally it has been employed to treat stomach upsets, jaundice, headaches, lack of appetite and nausea, while some people also swear by its hiccup-halting powers. Dill tea is thought to stimulate milk production in lactating mothers, while dipping fingers in it is said to help strengthen nails. Men can get a kick out of it too – in the past, athletes employed essence of dill as a muscle toner.

After a workout, take a (dill) leaf out of the Greeks' book and cover your head with it to induce sleep. Alternatively, the plant has some tasty kitchen uses: the flowers make a good addition to the pickle jar, and dill seeds (used whole or ground) are an excellent accompaniment to soups, fish, and vegetables.

EMOTIONAL

Aster

If only things had turned out differently.... This is the bittersweet
message of the aster, associated with love since Victorian times and
beyond. The tragic love that symbolizes these flowers is entwined in
the Greek myths. When Theseus volunteered to slay the Minotaur, he
promised his father Aegeus that he would return with white sails on his
boat if he succeeded in his quest. In a cruel twist of the kind epitomized
in Greek mythology, Theseus was made to forget his promise, and
when he returned with black sails raised, his father assumed the worst.
Shattered by grief, he killed himself. Where his blood flowed, the purple
aster grew.

The aster is indeed a delicate flower, fragile in appearance and love.
Its dainty heads were laid on the graves of French soldiers as a gesture
of loss and longing. It's a message also echoed in Robert Frost's 1915
poem "A Late Walk", which ends with the melancholy verse:

I end not far from my going forth
By picking the fading blue
Of the last remaining aster flower

Agapanthus

It's easy to understand why the statuesque agapanthus is so popular in paintings. Claude Monet was especially entranced by the flower, famously capturing its clusters of mauve blooms in his oil on canvas *Agapanthus*, which now hangs in New York's Museum of Modern Art.

More recently the native South African plant has been picked up by British pottery capital Stoke-on-Trent, inspiring a range of Portmeirion tableware. Depicted in monochrome, the flower's simple lines and understated glamour lend themselves well to the sophisticated dinner set. Potterheads can get a kick out of this plant; it's a feature of the Dursleys' front garden at 4 Privet Drive, and even Albus Dumbledore can't help commenting on their fine growth when he collects Harry.

Something from this flower's past echoes loudly through the passage of time. To the Victorians, it symbolized love and was often gifted to sweethearts in lieu of a love letter. Its very name, from the Greek *agápi* (meaning "love") and *anthos* ("flower"), makes it one of the most romantic blooms in the hothouse.

Dahlia

Sidelined inside cheap bouquets for too long, the dahlia is making
a forceful fashion comeback. The symmetry, brash colours and vast
number of shapes that saw it consigned to service-station forecourts for
decades, are now at the root of its renaissance. The catwalk collections of
Simone Rocha, Marni and Christopher Kane have all revived its allure.

It has almost as many emotional associations as it has separate species
(and there are 35 of those). From dignity to impending change, from
travel to a portent of betrayal, it has also picked up more macabre
connotations. "The Black Dahlia" was the nickname given to LA murder
victim Elizabeth Short in 1947, the violence of her death spawning a
slew of books, and TV and film works.

Perhaps it is the mystery – and sensationalism – still surrounding
this crime that inspired Givenchy's perfume Dahlia Noir. True dahlias
have no scent, leaving plenty of scope for olfactory fantasy. The result,
which has notes of pink pepper, mandarin, rose, peach, cedarwood,
sandalwood, vanilla and amber, is an imaginative homage to a Mexican
flower that is only just now enjoying its moment in the sun.

Anemone

Not for nothing is the balletic anemone also know as a "windflower". Even in a jug of water it will continue to twist and arch, its delicately collared face always turned expectantly towards the light. It is perhaps for this reason that we associate this delicate bloom with anticipation.

Over time the anemone has also become a symbol for unfading love, despite a relatively short vase life (just four to eight days). In Greek mythology it was the blood-red anemone that bereaved Aphrodite picked to preserve the memory of Adonis after he was brutally killed by a wild boar.

The flower has proved its longevity in design: the range of colours (red, pink, purple, blue and white) lends itself to a wide variety of depictions. William Morris's repeating motif of the flower, with a bird, was used on both textiles and wallpaper in the early 1880s. Many decades later, it's considered an iconic anemone-inspired work. What a fitting homage to this symbol of unfading love.

Delphinium

Poet Amy Lowell waxed lyrical about their "blue steeples", while fashion house Dior featured some 300,000 of them on a man-made mountain outside the Louvre for Paris Fashion Week 2015. With its long stems (some more than two metres tall) and full sleeves of smallish, open-faced flowers, the *delphinium*, or larkspur, lends itself well to statement design and rousing verse.

For all its spectacular good looks, the *delphinium* retains a relaxed, unpretentious quality. Designer Alexandre de Betak, who helped create the Dior installation, said the purple-blue perennial was chosen for just that attribute. "We wanted something that was impressive yet charming, and sometimes charming is simple," he explained to the *New York Times*.

The flower's larger-than-life physical characteristics have translated into an association with big-heartedness and fun. It is all the more surprising, then, that it is one of the most toxic of our garden plants.

Amaryllis

A Christmas plant *par excellence*, the decadent funnel-shaped flowers of the amaryllis are a sure way to brighten up the December home. They've recently replaced poinsettias as Britain's best-loved holiday bloom – a fact that should come as no surprise to anyone familiar with the flower's place in Greek mythology.

This is a plant that knows how to play the long game to get what it wants. Legend has it that timid shepherdess Amaryllis was so tortured by her love for the unattainable Alteo that she waited outside his door for 30 nights to win his affection. Every night, she pierced her heart with a golden arrow, and, where drops of her blood hit the ground, a single never-seen-before flower slowly formed. When Alteo finally opened the door and discovered her, he set eyes on these crimson petals – a sight so breath-taking that he forgot his misgivings and gathered her to his arms for a well-won kiss.

Maybe it's this story that had the Victorians associate the amaryllis with determination. Poinsettias offer instant gratification, sure, but the thrill of nursing an amaryllis bulb to flower is ultimately more satisfying.

Rose

"There is nothing more difficult for a truly creative painter than to paint a rose, because before he can do so he has first to forget all the roses that were ever painted."

The challenge set by Henri Matisse is one that has travelled across the creative spectrum, from poets and songwriters to designers and sculptors. It's not just the heady scent, velvety petals or gamut of colours. The rose subscribes to a certain school of coquetry, with its stem of prickles and propensity to harbour bees in the folds of its blooms. This dichotomy of dazzle and danger makes it the default symbol of passion.

But it is a complex flower that likes to play many roles; politically, the red rose stands as a symbol of both socialism and democracy, and as the national flower of England. Culturally, who knows how many hours have gone into the similes and still-life paintings, pop lyrics and perfumes that have popularized the rose?

"It is the time you have wasted for your rose that makes your rose so important," observes Antoine de Saint-Exupéry in *The Little Prince*.

Bouvardia

There's something of the Audrey Hepburn about the bouvardia. With its petite, starry flowers arranged in clusters on thin, branching stems, it has a gamine freshness and poise. The Victorians adored this about it, and saw the plant as the epitome of enthusiasm and zest for life. Hepburn herself would have summed up this attitude quite succinctly. "Pick the day," she once said. "Enjoy it – to the hilt. The day as it comes. People as they come..."

King Louis XIII's physician, Charles Bouvard, gave his name to this gentle flower. Superintendent of the Jardin des Plantes in Paris, he, more than most, believed in the restorative power of plants.

Available in soft shades of yellow, pink, white, salmon and red, the bouvardia is a great filler flower in arrangements, or as the focus in hand-tied bouquets. Its timeless appeal gives it massive versatility, but it works particularly well alongside roses for a dash of Victorian nostalgia.

Gladiolus

It shares its etymology (from the Latin word for "sword") with the armed combatants who fought in ancient Rome. But the stately stem of the gladiolus has more in common with those Colosseum stars than just a name, because it, too, has a fight on its hands to win over public opinion.

Australian comedian Barry Humphries reduced these funnel-shaped flowers to a symbol of phallic fun by having alter ego Dame Edna Everage throw gladioli ("gladdies") into the audience at the end of every show. Things hit a new low in 2014 when *Country Life* magazine listed planting them a sin for any reader aspiring to be a modern gentleman.

That's despite the flower's long positive associations with preparedness and strength. British singer Morrissey was a fan, brandishing them on stage or tucking a small bouquet in his back pocket. His The Smiths bandmate Johnny Marr later acknowledged it was flamboyant – but never fey – and claims the gladiolus became emblematic, even iconic.

This tenacious flower is here to stay. It's not only a symbol of love at first sight, but the flower favoured for fortieth wedding anniversaries, too.

EDIBLE

Sunflower

"Flaming flowers that brightly blaze" was how US singer Don McLean memorably described them in "Vincent", a track inspired by Van Gogh's series of sunflower still-life paintings. In London's National Gallery, postcards of the famous bouquet reportedly outsell all others in the bookshop, and the floor directly in front of the original is more scuffed and worn than any other section in the gallery.

Tall, with striking yellow heads, sunflowers are unmistakable, almost *too* highly coloured. They certainly succeed in attracting attention: even before they were committed to Van Gogh's canvas, the sunflower motif was a popular feature of stone and metalwork in the late nineteenth century Aesthetic Movement. They are head-turning in a very literal sense, too – tilting during the day to face the sun – and subsequently enjoy a long religious association as a symbol of the Christian soul.

Earlier civilizations had more practical uses for the sunflower. Some archaeologists believe it may have been farmed before corn. It was enjoyed among American Indian tribes, who ground the seed into flour for cakes and bread well before it was bottled in oil form for frying.

Lavender

Labelled "the ultimate multi-purpose plant" by the *Telegraph* in 2012, lavender has an impressive list of attributes. For more than 2,000 years, this hardy member of the mint family has been used for everything from mummifying bodies and protecting against plague, to relieving Queen Elizabeth I's migraines.

It's the heady combination of flavour and fragrance, however, that gives it such enduring appeal in the kitchen: honey, cakes and teas are the main foodstuffs to benefit, but the blooms can also be crystallized for use as delicate baking decorations, or even paired with cheese.

In the Elizabethan age, lavender was the traditional flower of love and featured in wedding bouquets because it was believed to bring luck in marriage. That good fortune started from Day 1 - the wedding night - with the flower's supposed aphrodisiac qualities seeing it regularly lining the bedsheets. So Queen Elizabeth ought never to have complained of having a headache.

Chrysanthemum

P.G. Wodehouse once likened a bad haircut to a chrysanthemum's pompom head, so it seems fitting that in some countries the flower should be associated with honesty – however unpalatable the truth may be. More commonly, in some places, incurve or white chrysanthemums are associated with death and grief, and are often found at the graveside.

Head east, and the flower assumes a wider significance. In China, where it is a symbol of nobility, it is popularly depicted on porcelain and in traditional ink and wash painting. Chrysanthemums are one of four plants making up the so-called "Four Gentlemen" of Chinese art, alongside the orchid, bamboo and plum blossom. In Japan, the flower inspired the national seal, is depicted on the front of passports and even lends its name to the highest knighthood – the Supreme Order of the Chrysanthemum. Each year the plant is celebrated in a Festival of Happiness.

When the chrysanthemum isn't being celebrated or painted, it's being consumed. It's sold in Asian markets for inclusion in teas (brewed with the dried flower buds), salads and soups.

Gentiana

The *gentiana*, also commonly known as gentian, isn't a flower that lets its diminutive stature stand in the way of getting noticed. Just a couple of inches tall, it turns heads with its piercingly blue petals instead – the Frank Sinatra of the alpine slopes. Ol' Blue Eyes would have approved; a 1906 advertisement published in the *Journal of Botany* claimed *gentiana* was popular with the ladies: "The only known flower in existence that exhilarates the heart and mind of the fair sex."

If you don't have time to study it on the ski slopes, you'll probably get better acquainted during the après-ski – the root of this plant makes a rather delicious distilled alcoholic beverage called gentian. An aromatic but bitter spirit, a sip or two is also thought to help settle digestive problems. Unfortunately for the people who make it, the plants have been placed under protection in Germany and Austria, and they can no longer be picked in the wild. Even grazing animals leave the *gentiana* alone, put off by its taste.

Safflower

With their punk spikes and vivid colours, a safflower's blooms are difficult to ignore. The ancient Egyptians were huge fans, and the expressive plant became a staple of garlands placed on mummies. Japan also embraced it: from early times it has featured in songs and poems, as well as facilitating traditional Japanese textile dyeing crafts. Later, East Indians used the safflower's crimson dye as their official "red tape" on legal documents.

It gives colour in the kitchen, too, its flowers lending dishes a light yellow-orange hue – alongside a subtle earthy flavour. For this reason, it is sometimes used as a cheap substitute for saffron and has earned the unfortunate nickname "bastard saffron" as a result.

Safflower comes into its own as an oil, however. Flavourless and, in this form, colourless, it is nutritionally similar to sunflower oil. Salad dressings, cooking oils and margarine production processes all depend heavily on it.

Carnation

Easy to grow and producing delectably frilly flowers, the carnation has become a staple of most floral arrangements and bouquets. It's far less familiar in the kitchen, however, which is a shame, because the petals are edible and can supply colour to salads and sophistication to cake decoration. Look to France for an alcoholic spin on the ingredient – here it's used in chartreuse, a liqueur that has been made by the Carthusian monks since 1737.

As well as in monasteries, the flower can be spied in Christian art too, having been depicted by Leonardo da Vinci in the late 1470s. His *Madonna of the Carnation* shows a young Virgin Mary with a naked baby Jesus on her lap. Her left hand holds the carnation, which is often interpreted as a healing motif.

Playwright Oscar Wilde imbued the carnation with still more symbolism when, for the first performance of his play *Lady Windermere's Fan* on 20th February 1892, he asked one of his actors – plus certain friends in the audience – to wear a green carnation in their buttonholes. It has since become emblematic of gay pride.

Nasturtium

"Easy on the eye" is a compliment we often use glibly, but if there's one flower that truly deserves such praise it's the fiery nasturtium. Its petals of bright oranges and deep reds bring welcome warm tones to the flower bed. Its edible credentials are equally impressive. While carrots may help you see in the dark, a bit of nasturtium in your diet could protect eyes from age-related macular degeneration and other common sight conditions. That's because it contains the highest amount of lutein (the so-called "eye vitamin") found in any edible plant.

The optical trivia doesn't stop there: nasturtiums are behind a strange spectacle known colloquially as "flashing flowers". This was discovered by the teenage daughter of Swedish botanist Carl Linnaeus, who observed that, especially at dusk, the petals seemed to emit tiny darts of light. Initially experts called it an electrical phenomenon, before realizing it was a reaction in the human eye caused by the contrast between the vivid orange flowers and their surrounding green leaves.

These leaves, like the flowers, have a strong peppery taste and can be ground with Parmesan and walnuts to make a delicious pesto.

Borage

The next summer day when you're sipping a fragrant cocktail, like Pimm's and lemonade, spare a thought for the humble borage, which has probably been replaced by a long sliver of cucumber peel in your glass. Traditionally, however, this blue, star-shaped bloom was the preferred garnish, imparting a similar flavour to that of its vegetable successor. It is a botanical favoured by many artisanal gin distillers.

Candied and made into a conserve, the flowers can also be put to medicinal use, and were historically given to people weakened by prolonged illness or susceptible to swooning. John Evelyn, the seventeenth-century English herbalist, clearly found the plant to be a useful placebo, wondering at its ability to "revive the hypochondriac".

Although found in most parts of Europe now, borage originally hails from Aleppo in Syria. You'll be able to distinguish it from close plant relatives by the distinctive beauty mark in its centre, made from a small cone of black "antlers". Furry stems and leaves are also a feature of borage – something thought to have inspired its name, which is derived from the Italian "borra", signifying hair or wool.

Viola

Walk past the pâtisserie windows of Toulouse, and you won't have to go far before spotting a viola inside. Petite, pretty and slightly perfumed, the viola has been candied here for centuries. Indeed, so strong is Toulouse's association with this flower, that it was once called "la cité de la violette". Once picked, the flowers are mummified in hot syrup, which is stirred until the sugar recrystallizes and dries. They're popular in cake decorations and are especially tasty paired with chocolate.

Nations around the world enjoy consuming the viola, helped by the fact that it is so easy to cultivate. Often confused with the pansy, the viola grows to a much smaller, compact size, making its five petals (four upswept, one pointing downward) more weather resistant. If you stoop low to breathe in its perfume, however, you may be in for a surprise. Violas contain the compound ionone, which temporarily disables the nose's ability to smell the flower. For that reason, parfumiers often describe the viola as having a "flirty" scent, because the fragrance teasingly comes and goes.

Rocket

The well-named rocket is mainly grown for its distinctive, nutty-flavoured leaves, which become more peppery as they mature. The flower is edible, too, and makes an appetizing garden snack eaten straight from the plant, or a pretty garnish on green salads.

Rocket flowers have four petals but otherwise vary considerably between species. Salad rocket blooms with creamy petals that house an intricate network of mauve capillaries just under their surface. Its close cousin the wild rocket is distinguished by its bright yellow heads, each petal about a centimetre long. It's commonly found growing as a weed on roadsides, where its tiny flashes of colour are often sadly unnoticed by drivers cruising past.

Both varieties are feminine and fragile, but that's not to say that the rocket is entirely genteel. Cultivated and eaten since Roman times, it was popular then as much for its aphrodisiac properties as pungent taste. Indeed, so well known was it as a sexual stimulant that the flower was allegedly banned in monasteries during the Middle Ages.

WILD

Astrantia

The astrantia, or masterwort, has earned the folk name "Hattie's pincushion" for the bundle of tiny flowerheads held aloft on fine stems. These meet at a central point on a ruff of pointed bracts, much like a sheriff's badge. That's no idle comparison for the astrantia: it has long symbolized strength, courage and protection, earning its stripes in the 400-odd years since it was introduced to foreign soils from its native central and eastern Europe.

Efforts to assimilate have often been fraught, however. Writing in *The English Flower Garden* in 1883, William Robinson bemoaned how the astrantia was "apt to over-run and exhaust the soil", suggesting it should be relegated to "the back part of the shrubbery".

But the years since have been kind to this most photogenic of plants, with gardeners rushing to hybridize ever-showier forms. Like so many flowers, though, it isn't just a pretty face: the astrantia has also been prized for its medicinal benefits.

Yarrow

Much like the daisy – "He loves me, he loves me not..." – the yarrow is a bit of an oracle. Tickle the inside of your nose with its leaf and, according to folklore, you'll be able to divine the feelings of the person you desire:

Yarroway, yarroway, bear a white blow,
If my love love me, my nose will bleed now.

At the very least, the flow of blood was thought to relieve headaches. More commonly, however, yarrow is used to staunch rather than prompt bleeding. Its Latin name, *achillea*, derives from the myth that Achilles was given the flower by the centaur Chiron to help him treat soldiers' wounds on the battlefield.

Whatever use you put it to, yarrow offers great value in the garden, with long-flowering, flattish clusters of pretty blooms that are beloved by insects. When crushed, both leaves and flowers have a pungent but not unpleasant, smell. Among the host of florid monikers this flower has earned, one in particular could be a nod to its unusual smell: old man's pepper. It's certainly an apt name for a plant that was once employed as snuff.

Phlox

From the Greek word meaning "flame", phlox is certainly a trailblazer. In her 1916 book *My Garden*, horticultural writer Louise Beebe Wilder said of one variety: "This plant is a native, and with true American perspicacity and enterprise has forged his way from magenta obscurity to the most prominent place in the floral world."

Part of its success lies in the flower's reputation for being a bit of an all-rounder. It grows well in the wild but was equally amenable to cottage garden life when it was brought to Europe from America in the 1700s. Tamed, its old-fashioned blooms form little communities of colour in the flower bed, from pure white, to red, and everything in-between.

In the language of flowers, phlox speaks of solidarity. "Our souls are united" or "We think alike" is the message you're giving someone by presenting a posy of phlox. Clearly, this lends itself well to wedding celebrations, and the flower has also been used in love potions and to encourage disparate groups of people to work together harmoniously.

Helenium

Even if you've never seen one, a quick glance through some of the
names given to helenium varieties will conjure some idea of the velvety,
flame-coloured ruff of petals it's recognized for. From Feuersiegel ("fiery
lightening bolt") to Flammenspiel ("dancing flames"), and Kleiner Fuchs
("little fox") to Rubinzwerg ("ruby dwarf"), the deep reds, rusts and golds
give a rush of colour to wild meadows and well-kept lawns alike.

The petals are arranged like gap-teeth around a central yellow cone and
can be seen from August to November in thickets across North America.
Members of the *aster* family, heleniums are also notoriously hardy, and
can reportedly withstand temperatures as low as -40°C. They also face
up to hungry livestock fairly well; the animals are usually put off by the
unfriendly dose of toxic glucoside heleniums contain. This has been
less of a deterrent for humans – in the past, dried leaves were used to
make snuff. Native Americans believed the sneezes it elicited could rid a
person of evil spirits – hence the funny, colloquial name of sneezeweed.

Laceflower

For the amateur gardener, the laceflower (*ammi majus*) offers a tempting combination of low maintenance and high returns (quite literally, because it can grow to more than two metres tall). From afar, it looks as if the slender, branched stems have reached so far skywards as to have caught wisps of clouds. Come closer, though, and you'll see how each large, round bloom is actually made up of scores of delicate white florets clustered together and resembling fine lacework.

As befits a wild flower, growing laceflower at home has the advantage of bringing the rest of the countryside closer, too. The plant will attract "good" insects into the garden, including hoverflies and butterflies, and it's also a great choice for landscaping, too.

And, because this is a generous flower, its utility extends beyond the horticultural and into herbal medicine. Ancient Egyptians found it helpful for treating skin complaints, and to this day it is considered useful as a cardiac tonic for angina and palpitations.

Geraldton wax

Geraldton wax (*chamelaucium uncinatum*) is a most precious Australian export. It thrives in its home state of Western Australia where, hugging roads and carpeting exposed embankments, it receives just enough sunshine, drainage and benign neglect to bud and bloom from late winter well into summer.

This is a flower that doesn't like fuss. Long has it tested gardeners who have removed it from the wild and tried growing it in the suburbs instead. As a 1967 issue of *Australian Plants* attested: "While there are certainly more difficult species of Australian plants to establish, there are few with such a record of frustration."

Persistence pays off though, because these flowers can be spectacular and bring a rare splash of colour in early spring when there are few rival blooms about. The petals have a heavy, waxy texture and, in the wild at least, are commonly white with a mauve tinge. Purple and reds are propagated commercially, where they make a long-lasting cut flower in bouquets.

Cornflower

Much like George Bernard Shaw's fictional Eliza Doolittle, the cornflower has risen from humble origins to become the surprise toast of elite society. These days you're more likely to see it as a boutonnière at a royal banquet than as weed on a farmer's field. In fact, the overuse of herbicides has slowly destroyed the cornflower's natural habitat, and the last half century has seen its home shrink from more than 250 sites in the UK to just three.

As a fashion accessory, however, it continues to flourish, helped by its handy size and electric-blue tones. It was John F. Kennedy's favourite flower, and his son Jack Jr. wore it in the lapel of his midnight-blue suit and white piqué waistcoat at his 1996 wedding, in tribute to his father.

Cornflowers appeal equally to feminine sensibilities. In E.M. Forster's novel, *A Room With A View*, the two spinster sisters, the Miss Alans, are obsessed with the flowers. Cornflowers are also famously used in some Lady Grey blends of tea: the startlingly blue petals pop beautifully against the large black tea leaves. It's this fantastic colour that has made the cornflower prized for its pigment over the years.

EXOTIC

Sea holly

Tough as nails, sea holly is a seaside staple. Everything about its striking architecture shows how centuries of poor soil and bracing ocean breezes have put it on permanent defence, from the thimble-like cone of flowers at the centre, to the spiked leaves forming a ninja throwing star around it. Even its play of colours (from the blue greens of weathered bronze to metallic silvers) suggests an armoury within.

For William Robinson, the great Irish gardener of the Edwardian period, this prickliness was what made sea holly so perfect. He insisted its beauty was not surpassed by any other plant. The poet Jean Sprackland also delights in its non-traditional features, using it as a symbol of steely love in her poem "Sea Holly". Describing the bouquet she gifts her partner, she purposely avoids "the usual pale translucent blooms/with the rot already in them". Instead, she chooses flowers that are "fierce and electric... they blaze in the storm like blue torches".

Bird of paradise

It's easy to see why the magnificent *strelitzia* is more popularly known as the "bird of paradise" in its native South Africa. From afar, the vivid orange sepals look like tufts of bright feathers, the spathe a sharp beak. Real birds revel in the confusion, visiting the flowers often to perch on these stately thrones. Their weight releases pollen onto their feet, which they inadvertently carry to the next flower, thereby pollinating the species.

The *strelitzia* has associations with liberty and good perspective. It is fitting, then, that anti-apartheid leader and former South African president Nelson Mandela lent his name to a rare strain of dusky yellow *strelitzia*, which was branded Mandela's Gold in his honour.

Flame lily

If it's a showstopper you're after in the garden, look no further than the aptly-monikered flame lily, a climbing vine with six elongated yellow and pink or red petals that wrinkle with maturation to resemble a flickering candle.

The *gloriosa superba*, to give the plant its proper name, is unquestionably the femme fatale of the flower world. Its seductive looks hide a horrific secret: all parts of this plant, especially the tubers, are extremely toxic. Ingestion can cause death, and the flower has been used to commit suicide and murder and even to induce abortions in the past.

Zimbabwe is happy to overlook all this and has made the flame lily the country's national flower. When then-Princess Elizabeth visited in 1947, she was gifted a diamond brooch in the shape of this striking plant. However, in these parts it has become a victim of its own success. Zimbabwean newspaper reports recently warned it is facing extinction because of illegal harvesting and trade. It is now a protected plant.

Guernsey lily

There's an air of frivolity about the *nerine sarniensis* that is hard not to find endearing. Perhaps this comes from the jostling funnel-shaped florets that make up its bright flowerhead, or the way, as a journalist in the *Independent* put it, the fleshy stem "leans slightly, but intently, towards you, like an over-eager party guest".

Whatever the reason, this exotic creature – native to South Africa – brings welcome cheer to the gardens of the northern hemisphere, too. Nowhere more so than the Channel Islands, which gave the plant its name when a ship of bulbs bound for the Netherlands was shipwrecked off the coast of Guernsey. The genus label, *nerine*, derives from the sea-nymphs (Nereids) of Greek mythology that protected stricken sailors, while the epithet *sarniensis* refers to the Island of Sarnia, the Roman name for Guernsey.

Brunia

The brunia isn't showing its age one bit. Despite pre-dating the first primates (but not quite as old as dinosaurs), its silver-grey spherical berries look oddly futuristic, and the plant towers some two to three metres high in the Western Cape of South Africa.

The flowers themselves are small and white, but grouped into flat, rounded heads. Yellow stamens flare out, lending the bloom the appearance of a little firecracker. At the centre sits a drop of purple, sticky nectar, which lures a steady queue of sunbirds, ants, wasps, bees and beetles.

Sadly, research shows that this unusual plant may slowly be heading towards extinction, with many varieties difficult to propagate from seed and successfully cultivate. Let's hope the brunia has the will to live – its novel colour and texture have made it an increasingly popular choice for bridal bouquets and as a table decoration. There is undoubtedly something quite Christmassy about it, too; the leaves on its stem look like short pine needles, which are festively topped with clusters of miniature bauble-like heads.

Chocolate cosmos

Like something straight out of Willy Wonka's factory, the chocolate cosmos is so-named for its light vanillin fragrance, redolent of a freshly unwrapped candy bar. The velvety red-brown flowers complete this sweetly edible impression. It's almost as rare as Roald Dahl's fictional golden-ticketed treat, too; with none left in the wild, it has to be carefully propagated by hand.

How fitting that this curious plant should hail from the home of chocolate itself – Mexico. Unfortunately no part is edible, so one has to be content with enjoying its delicious aroma in bouquet cuttings or the flower bed.

Chocolate cosmos will bloom right up until autumn, when its deep colour perfectly complements the earthy tones of the fallen leaves around it. Its sensuous hue makes the flower a popular Valentine's gift, from which it has perhaps earned its symbolism for a love greater than anyone else can muster.

TOXIC

Tulip

Would you ever pay a small fortune for the perfect bunch of flowers? Such was the demand for tulips in seventeenth-century Holland that some people were prepared to spend ten times the annual salary of a skilled craftsman to get their hands on a single rare bulb. "Tulip mania", as it became known, had gripped the nation. The economic phenomenon inspired Alexandre Dumas's great novel *The Black Tulip*, and vases of the flowers were a mainstay of Dutch still-life painting. Judith Leyster's tulip from her *Tulip Book* (1643) is a memorable example.

Elegant and never short of confidence, the tulip had made its entrance. Boasting more than 3,000 species, it keeps us fascinated to this day. It has staggering symbolic versatility, too, changing meaning with every hue – from a statement of enduring love (cream) to an appeal for trust (red).

Spare a thought for those early Dutch traders who staked their fortune on the flower, however – and lost it when the market ultimately crashed. Their modern counterparts live with the occupational hazard of skin allergies from the toxins contained in the stems, leaves and blooms. That pop of colour comes at a price...

Hydrangeas display an aura of impetuous decadence, with their dense billowing heads of pink, blue or white petals, which change colour as if on a whim. They curried such favour with the Victorians, perhaps because their frilly fullness was the perfect expression of the excess in design that was then *de rigueur* in everything from fashion to furniture. Pattern designer Lindsay Butterfield's 1896 "Hydrangea" wallpaper was an ostentatious repeat of pink hydrangea and foliage.

But this revered beauty can be deadly. Hydrangeas are charged with hydrogen cyanide (or prussic acid), which can cause a slow and painful death when consumed in large quantities. More moderate consumption, however, has proved irresistible to a certain group of French fans. In 2014 the so-called "gang des hortensias" ("hydrangea gang") was at the centre of a police hunt after ripping off the delicate heads in dozens of ornamental gardens to smoke as a cheap legal alternative to cannabis.

Iris germanica

This European hybrid boasts a dizzying range of colours, from jet black to bright white. In fact, iris means "rainbow" in Greek. It is also the name of the Greek goddess said to link the deities to humanity. As a messenger, her sacred flower was often planted on the graves of women whose grieving husbands hoped the gesture would take their souls to the Elysian Fields.

Although it is toxic, the iris has been used for medicinal purposes and in the manufacture of perfume. The flower itself has no smell, but the root can be cleaned and dried and, to this day, brings a warm, earthy scent to fragrances as diverse as Chanel Nº19, Prada's Infusion d'Iris, Les Senteurs' Iris Oriental and Guerlain's iconic Après L'Ondée. One reviewer memorably likened the latter to "being sprinkled in baby powder and cuddled".

A stylized version of the iris (although some say lily) is thought to be the inspiration for the fleur-de-lis, the religious, political, dynastic and artistic emblem prevalent in French heraldry.

Calla lily

In May 2015 a painting of a white calla lily sold for close to a staggering $9-million. The work of American modernist Georgia O'Keeffe, it was the headline lot of a sale of US art at Sotheby's. With its sweeping wave-like spathe, it isn't hard to work out what attracted the buyer to the subject, nor why O'Keeffe herself regularly used this flower as a motif in her paintings. In fact, so enamoured was she with this canvas that she kept it in her personal collection until her death in 1986.

Hailing from southern Africa, the calla lily comes in a range of other colours too, from mango to royal purple. It is not a true lily, but its beauty has nevertheless won admirers outside of the art world. It appears on the Easter Lily badge worn by Irish Republicans as a symbol of remembrance for those who died as a result of the 1916 Easter Rising, and it's also the national flower of Saint Helena.

Other countries are more wary of the calla lily, however. In Western Australia it is classified as a toxic weed because ingestion can cause swelling of the mouth and throat, and stomach pain. In nature, beauty frequently warns of danger.

Euphorbia fulgens

Despite being a close relative of the poinsettia, the only thing this pair has in common is a propensity to be handed out at Christmas. At least in Mexico, that is, from where this long, elegantly curved plant originates. Its branches are decorated with pointed leaves and small rounded flowers, often a festive red, but also orange, yellow, pink and white.

An altogether less jovial aspect of the *euphorbia fulgens*, or scarlet-plume, is its toxicity. Perhaps the spear-like leaf form is a giveaway. Tear one open, and you'll find a sap inside that can sometimes irritate the skin. To be on the safe side, many florists will seal the cut end by dipping it in alcohol or even cauterizing it. The mild poison, however, has not done anything to diminish the plant's popularity in wedding bouquets, where its vivid colours can really help a bride to stand out from the crowd.

Monkshood

No prizes for guessing how *aconitum* got its common names "monkshood", "devil's helmet", "old wife's hood" and, in Scandinavia, "October stormhat". This furtive-looking flower – a relation of the delphinium – has cylindrical petals that form a distinctive cowl, commonly purple but also blue, white, yellow or pink.

This cloak-and-dagger look serves the flower well, because monkshood is one of the most toxic plants in the garden. Canadian actor Andre Noble died after accidentally ingesting it during a hiking trip in 2004, while it hit headlines again in 2009 when a high-profile murder case revealed death had been caused by lacing a curry with it. More recently, in 2014, a gardener collapsed and died after apparently handling it at work.

Thankfully, monkshood has such an unpleasant taste that cases of accidental poisoning are rare. Not so in popular culture, however, where instances abound of gruesome ends by misadventure – and foul play. TV crime series all over the world have featured the plant in their plots.

Catalogue of flowers

Here are all 50 of the flowers in the order in which they appear in the book. They have been reproduced to scale on the following pages in order to give an indication of their relative sizes.

Stargazer lily: page 10
(Lilium "stargazer")

Cockscomb: page 12
(Celosia cristata)

Lady's mantle: page 14
(Alchemilla mollis)

Cyclamen: page 16
(Cyclamen)

Dandelion: page 18
(Taraxacum officinale)

Snapdragon: page 20
(Antirrhinum)

Clematis: page 24
(Clematis)

Matriciana chamomilla: page
26 (Matriciana chamomilla)

Physalis: page 28
(Physalis)

Lily of the valley: page 30
(Convallaria majalis)

Snowberry: page 32
(Symphoricarpos)

Dill: page 34
(Anethum graveolens)

Aster: page 38
(Aster)

Agapanthus: page 40
(Agapanthus)

Dahlia: page 42
(Dahlia)

Anemone: page 44
(Anemone)

Delphinium: page 46
(Delphinium)

Amaryllis: page 48
(Hippeastrum)

Rose: page 50
(Rosa)

Bouvardia: page 52
(Bouvardia)

Gladiolus: page 54
(Gladiolus)

Sunflower: page 58
(Helianthus)

Lavender: page 60
(Lavandula)

Chrysanthemum: page 62
(Chrysanthemum)

Gentiana: page 64
(Gentiana)

Safflower: page 66
(Carthamus tinctorius)

Carnation: page 68
(Dianthus caryophyllus)

Nasturtium: page 70
(Tropaeolum majus)

Borage: page 72
(Borago officinalis)

Viola: page 74
(Viola)

Rocket: page 76
(Eruca sativa)

Astrantia: page 80
(Astrantia)

Yarrow: page 82
(Achillea millefolium)

Phlox: page 84
(Phlox)

Helenium: page 86
(Helenium autumnale)

Laceflower: page 88
(Ammi majus)

Geraldton wax: page 90
(Chamelaucium uncinatum)

Cornflower: page 92
(Centaurea cyanus)

Sea holly: page 96
(Eryngium maritimum)

Bird of paradise: page 98
(Strelitzia)

Flame lily: page 100
(Gloriosa superba)

Guernsey lily: page 102
(Nerine sarniensis)

Brunia: page 104
(Brunia)

Chocolate cosmos: page 106
(Cosmos atrosanguineus)

Tulip: page 110
(Tulipa)

Hydrangea: page 112
(Hydrangea)

Iris germanica: page 114
(Iris germanica)

Calla lily: page 116
(Zantedeschia aethiopica)

Euphorbia fulgens: page 118
(Euphorbia fulgens)

Monkshead: page 120
(Aconitum)

Acknowledgements

This lovely book now finished, it is good to reflect on the important work and belief from all the members of the team.

The journey started with Richard's original idea. Then came the crafting and seeing it become a beautiful reality.

The enthusiasm and skill from our editor at Quadrille, Céline Hughes, and our art director Nicola Ellis, have been amazing.

Personally too, I owe full credit to my team: Emily Lutyens and Sarah Henshaw. Both are talented, loyal and always there when ideas, decisions, research and words needed more than one brain working on them. I am grateful to them both.

Finally, I must thank my family, Robert and Matt; their patience with my obsessive work nature is long-standing and pretty impressive. I hope that they, and you, enjoy every page of this book. It is a joy to be able to share it.

Thank you.

Jane

The genesis of this book goes as far back as 1978 when my mother opened a flower shop. As a youngster, I was intrigued by the colours and textures.

Many years on, Jane Field-Lewis and I travelled around the country shooting for her various beautiful books. The idea for this book was born somewhere between Leicester and London, I think – a book simply of flowers, with some text to inform, keeping it nice and simple.

I have to say a huge thank you to my co-author Jane – her passion and drive are such rare things in a person. I also have to thank my "photo" dads, Jeff Robins and Seamus Ryan. I wouldn't be who I am or where I am without them. Further thanks to the amazing Michi Kanatschnig from McQueens whose botanical expertise was invaluable.

Thanks to Nicola Ellis at Quadrille, the lady who kept me sane during the long days of post-production; and to Céline Hughes, our editor who guided us with a patient and sensitive hand.

Finally, thanks to my wife, Helen, and children, Louis and Scarlett. Their love and support are in everything I do. To them I dedicate the images in this book.

Richard

Publishing Director: Sarah Lavelle

Creative Director: Helen Lewis

Senior Editor: Céline Hughes

Senior Designer: Nicola Ellis

Design Assistant: Emily Lapworth

Photographer: Richard Maxted

Production: Vincent Smith, Tom Moore

First published in 2016 by
Quadrille Publishing
Pentagon House
52–54 Southwark Street
London SE1 1UN
www.quadrille.co.uk

Quadrille is an imprint of Hardie Grant
www.hardiegrant.com.au

Text © 2016 Jane Field-Lewis
Photography © 2016 Richard Maxted
Design and layout © 2016 Quadrille Publishing

Cataloguing in Publication Data: a catalogue record for this book is available from the British Library.

ISBN: 978 184949 789 3

Printed in China

The authors and publisher would like to thank McQueens for their kind donation of flowers for the book. Special thanks go to botanical advisor Michi Kanatschnig for invaluable guidance and help.

McQueens
229 Cambridge Heath Road
Bethnal Green
London E2 0EL
mcqueens.co.uk